Great Historic Debates and Speeches™

# THE CALHOUN-RANDOLPH DEBATE ON THE EVE OF THE WAR OF 1812

## A PRIMARY SOURCE INVESTIGATION

Jennifer Silate

rosen central
**Primary Source**™

The Rosen Publishing Group, Inc., New York

Published in 2005 by The Rosen Publishing Group, Inc.
29 East 21st Street, New York, NY 10010

First Edition

Unless otherwise attributed, all quotes in this book are excerpted from the congressional records of John Randolph's address to Congress on December 10, 1811, and John Calhoun's address to Congress on December 12, 1811.

### Library of Congress Cataloging-in-Publication Data

Silate, Jennifer.
The Calhoun-Randolph debate on the eve of the War of 1812: a primary source investigation / by Jennifer Silate.
    p. cm.—(Great historic debates and speeches)
Includes bibliographical references and index.
Contents: The making of great men—On the path to war—Randolph opposes the push for war—Calhoun defends the war resolutions—The war years—After the war.
ISBN 1-4042-0150-5 (lib. bdg.)
1. United States—History—War of 1812—Juvenile literature. 2. United States—Politics and government—1801–1815—Juvenile literature. 3. Calhoun, John C. (John Caldwell), 1782–1850—Juvenile literature. 4. Randolph, John 1773–1833—Juvenile literature. 5. Legislators—United States—Biography—Juvenile literature. [1. United States—History—War of 1812. 2. United States—Politics and government—1801–1815. 3. Calhoun, John C. (John Caldwell), 1782–1850. 4. Randolph, John 1773–1833. 5. Legislators.]
I. Title. II. Series.
E357.S55 2005
973.5'2—dc22

                                                                        2003025460

*Manufactured in the United States of America*

**Cover images:** Left: A portrait of John C. Calhoun. Right: A portrait of John Randolph.

# CONTENTS

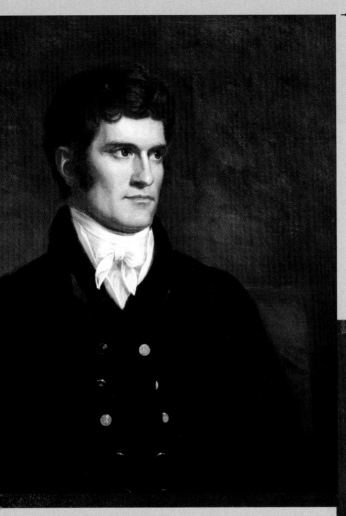

 John C. Calhoun sat for this portrait in 1822, eleven years after he made a powerful case for going to war with England primarily over British violation of American shipping rights. The painting was done by Charles Bird King.

This portrait of John Randolph was painted by John Wesley Jarvis in 1811. It was in that year that Randolph made an impassioned address to Congress in which he urged his colleagues not to go to war with England.

# INTRODUCTION

Many great debates have shaped the United States over the years. From America's earliest days, disagreements in government have led to debates that have changed America's laws and defined its actions. In the first years after the Revolutionary War (1775–1883), the leaders of the United States often disagreed about how the young country should be run. The disagreements were mostly played out between the two parties that controlled the government: the Federalists and the Republicans.

The first president of the United States, George Washington, was a Federalist. The Federalists held a majority in Congress until 1800. While in power, the Federalists established a number of institutions and policies to build the new nation. They started a national bank and made efforts to keep the country safe from other countries. The Federalists also believed that the best way to avoid war was to be prepared for it. Accordingly, they worked to make the army larger, to rebuild the navy, and to construct and repair forts along the East Coast. The Federalists also signed treaties with England to make trade easier and to keep peace with the powerful country.

The Jay Treaty was one of the most important of these records. In 1794, Chief Justice John Jay was sent to England to discuss problems between the United States and Great Britain. At that time, Great Britain was at war with France, and it was seizing American ships that traded with French-owned islands in the Caribbean. Great Britain also restricted trade between the United States and British colonies in the West Indies. These actions angered Americans.

Jay hoped the United States would get repayment for the slaves, goods, and ships that Great Britain had seized, be able to trade freely with the British West Indies, and get British troops to withdraw from American land in the West.

Great Britain agreed to leave the West and to pay for American ships and goods it had taken. However, the British continued to heavily restrict America's trade with the West Indies. America also had to pay British merchants for debts from before the Revolutionary War. In addition, Jay agreed to several trade restrictions on neutral ships during wartime.

The Jay Treaty outraged many people. The Republicans did not like it because they felt that it greatly limited the United States' rights. France also disliked the treaty. France, which had backed the United States during the Revolutionary War against England, felt that the Jay Treaty violated various agreements that it had with the United States. In retaliation, French warships started capturing American merchant ships and goods in 1798. The United States responded by sending its new navy to stop them. The U.S. Navy captured more than 100 French privateers (private ships that worked for the government to capture enemy ships). It also recovered more than seventy American ships. This standoff was called the Quasi-War.

In 1800, the Quasi-War ended, and the United States was at peace with France. Former treaties with France were ended, too. Despite the success of the Quasi-War, the Federalists were losing popularity with Americans. High taxes to support the Quasi-War and the Jay Treaty were very unpopular. Many people thought that the Federalists' foreign policies were too pro-British.

In 1801, Thomas Jefferson, a Republican, became president. The Republicans worked to lower government spending, especially military spending, and to lower taxes. They reduced the size of the army and stopped work on new ships for the navy. In the first years of Jefferson's presidency, England and France were still at war. However, the United States continued to trade with both. The American economy grew fast as trade increased.

The good times did not last very long. In the early 1800s, tensions rose again

Thomas Jefferson was the third president of the United States. As president, his most significant achievement was the completion of the Louisiana Purchase, which doubled the size of the young nation.

between England, France, and the United States. Again, American ships were being seized and more trade restrictions were put on American merchants. The United States opened negotiations with France and England. Talk of war started after the first round of negotiations failed. A new debate was beginning over what to do about the problems between the United States and the two powerful countries. Eventually, the debate settled on going to war with Great Britain. In the forefront of this debate were two men—John C. Calhoun and John Randolph. Their ideas, goals, and concerns helped to shape America then and now.

## CHAPTER 1

# THE MAKING OF GREAT MEN

The men at the center of the 1811 debate over going to war with Great Britain were both Republicans. However, they were very different. One was a youthful and confident freshman congressman from rural South Carolina; the other was a frail middle-aged seasoned politician with a well-bred, urban background.

## John C. Calhoun

John Caldwell Calhoun was born on March 18, 1782, near Abbeville, South Carolina. At the time, the Revolutionary War was still being fought in America. British troops and those who supported them, called Tories, killed several members of his family. John Calhoun's family lived in what was then called the backcountry of South Carolina. John's father, who was named Patrick, his grandmother, and two of John's uncles moved there in 1756. Only about 7,000 whites and 300 slaves lived in the backcountry at that time. Native Americans also lived in the area. Often white settlers and the Native Americans fought each other.

Patrick Calhoun soon made a name for himself in the backcountry. He successfully fought Native Americans and was chosen to lead a patrol to keep settlers safe from attack. He became a surveyor, and he helped hundreds of people in the area. Patrick Calhoun also founded a church and worked as a justice of the peace. He was even elected to the state legislature. Patrick Calhoun was not among the richest people of South Carolina, but he was better off than most in the backcountry. He had many acres of farmland, several slaves, and a two-story house.

John Calhoun worked on the family farm from a very young age. He was the fourth son of the Calhoun family. Despite being one of the youngest, it was he whom his father had singled out to receive an education. Patrick Calhoun wanted John to follow in his footsteps and have a successful public career.

When John Calhoun was about thirteen, he was sent to study with his brother-in-law, Moses Waddel. Soon after John began his studies, his father and sister died within a few weeks of each other. After his sister's death, John was left with his brother-in-law, 50 miles (81 kilometers) from home. During this time, he read everything he could from Waddel's library. After three months, however, his mother, worried about his health, brought him home. Once home, John was placed in charge of the family farm. At the time of his death, John's father had owned 1,200 acres (486 hectares) and about thirty slaves. John was now in charge of it all.

For the next four years, John made all of the decisions for the farm. When he was eighteen years old, John's brothers asked him if he was interested in continuing his education as his father had wanted. John decided that he did, and two of his brothers ran the farm. On May 14, 1801, less than two months before John Calhoun left for school, his mother died.

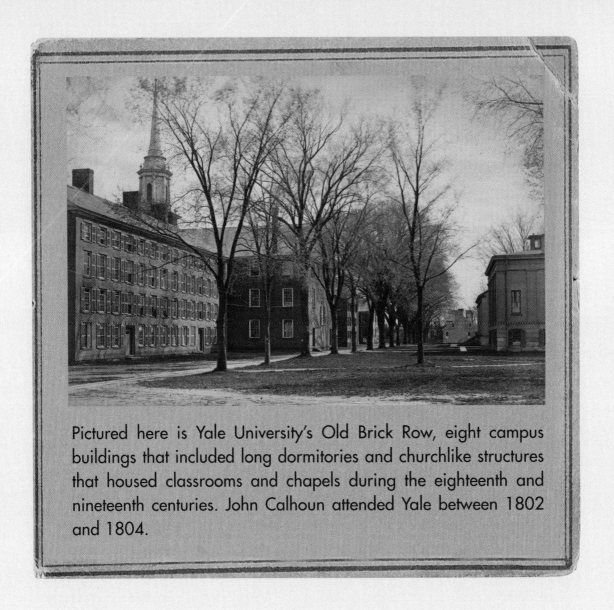

Pictured here is Yale University's Old Brick Row, eight campus buildings that included long dormitories and churchlike structures that housed classrooms and chapels during the eighteenth and nineteenth centuries. John Calhoun attended Yale between 1802 and 1804.

Calhoun returned to Moses Waddel's school. He worked hard, and in 1802, he started as a junior at Yale University. There, Calhoun sharpened his debating skills. He even debated the college president on at least two occasions. His classmates looked up to him, and the college president said that he had the skills to someday become president of the United States. Calhoun graduated from Yale in 1804 and entered the De Sauss and Ford law firm as a student that December. In May 1805, he traveled to Connecticut to study at the Litchfield Law School. Again, fellow students were amazed by Calhoun's debating skills and his ability to remember and use facts.

Calhoun returned to South Carolina in late 1806 and passed the bar exam in 1807. He had completed his schooling and had become a lawyer. However, Calhoun did not enjoy being a lawyer. He soon switched to politics. In 1808, he was elected to the South Carolina House of Representatives. Two years later, he was elected to the United States House of Representatives, replacing his uncle Joseph, who had retired. In 1811, John Calhoun left for Washington. He was about to fulfill his father's wishes as he started his career in the United States Congress. One of the first people that Calhoun faced in debate in Congress was John Randolph.

# John Randolph of Roanoke

John Randolph was born on June 2, 1773. He came from a wealthy and well-educated family in Cawsons, Virginia. Unlike Calhoun, who did not have many books at home and went elsewhere to study, Randolph grew up with a large library in his home. His father died when he was young, and his mother married a poet named St. George Tucker. Randolph's mother encouraged him to read and to practice giving speeches. Randolph loved reading, but he disliked school. He preferred to learn on his own. He went to several schools for short amounts of time. He spent a year at Princeton University, almost two years at Columbia University, and a few weeks at the College of William and Mary. Randolph also studied law with his uncle Edmund Randolph from 1790 to 1793.

When Randolph was about nineteen years old, he got very ill. No one knows exactly what the illness was, but it haunted him for the rest of his life. His body was very thin and weak. Sometimes, particularly as he got older, the illness even affected his mind. Despite these problems, Randolph had a long career in politics.

This is an engraving of Roanoke, the country home of John Randolph. Born in Cawsons, Virginia, he was known as John Randolph of Roanoke to distinguish him from relatives also named John. Randolph was buried at Roanoke when he died in 1833. His remains were later removed to Hollywood Cemetery in Richmond, Virginia.

In 1801, only two years after first being elected to Congress, he became the majority leader of the House of Representatives under President Thomas Jefferson.

Randolph did not trust people with power, and he hated corruption. Randolph held very strong opinions, and in 1805, he clashed with Jefferson and the Republican Party. Leaders in Georgia had been bribed to sell land at a low price. The public was upset by this deal. They elected new legislators, who overturned the deal. The companies who had bought the land asked the federal government to pay them for their losses. President Jefferson wanted to pay the companies part of what they wanted from the U.S. Treasury.

Randolph was outraged. He felt that it was wrong to pay the companies anything since the deal had been corrupt. He also did not think the federal government should interfere with what the people of the state wanted. Randolph clashed with Jefferson on several other occasions in the next year. He often sided with the Federalists, but he would never join them.

Randolph soon became alienated from the Republican Party. He fought for what he believed whether it was popular or not. Randolph worked to defend agriculture in America and the ways of the South. He

# THE TERTIUM QUIDS: A THIRD WAY

After John Randolph's break from Jefferson, he formed an opposition group of Southerners called the Tertium Quids. *Tertium quid* means "third something" in Latin. Randolph and his supporters were neither Jeffersonian Republicans nor Federalists; they were a third party. The Tertium Quids were also called the Old Republicans. They were for states' rights above all else—an idea that was becoming the old way of thinking in Congress. Randolph led the Tertium Quids for most of his life.

further separated himself from other congressmen through his odd dress and behavior. He often wore a long, flowing cape and even brought his dogs with him to congressional meetings. Despite his oddness, people respected his debating skills.

In 1811, a new batch of congressmen met for the twelfth Congress. These men had their own ideas of how the country should be run and were not afraid to defend them. They were nationalists who wanted to take the country in new directions, to which John Randolph was mostly opposed. John Calhoun quickly became one of the leaders of these men. It was then that the debate between John Randolph and John Calhoun began.

## CHAPTER 2

# ON THE PATH TO WAR

During the late 1700s and the early 1800s, the United States benefited greatly from the warring between England and France. A revolution had been under way in France, and a revolutionary government replaced the monarchy. In 1793, the revolutionary government executed King Louis XVI and Queen Marie Antoinette. Great Britain was opposed to this action and started fighting against the French revolutionary government. The situation grew worse in 1799, when France was ruled by a military general named Napoléon Bonaparte. Bonaparte warred with many countries in an effort to take them over. In response, England worked to block trade with France. England stopped French ships from trading with England's West Indian colonies, a major resource for the French. It also tried to stop other countries from trading with France.

However, the United States transported goods between the West Indies and France, supplying the French with what they needed. This angered England. It did not want France to get supplies from the West Indies through the United

States. It also wanted a share of the profits from trade with France. British ships began seizing American merchant ships that were suspected of transporting goods from the West Indies to France. Between 300 and 400 ships were seized.

# The *Chesapeake* Affair

British ships were also stopping American ships and taking sailors who they thought might have come from the British army. One-quarter of the sailors on American ships were British, many of whom had become American citizens. About 6,000 American citizens were taken from American ships. They were put on British warships and forced to fight the French. The British even entered American waters to take ships and men.

President Jefferson sent James Monroe and William Pinckney to England to persuade its government to stop taking American ships and sailors. Monroe and Pinckney signed a treaty with England in which England agreed to allow Americans to trade West Indian goods with France if they paid England a small duty. However, the British would not promise to stop taking sailors that it claimed had deserted from the British army. England needed all its sailors to fight Napoléon.

When the treaty arrived in Washington, President Jefferson refused to give it to the Senate to be ratified, or approved. After the rejection of the Monroe-Pinckney Treaty, relations with England got worse.

On June 22, 1807, the captain of the British ship HMS *Leopard* requested permission for his men to board the American ship *Chesapeake* to look for deserters from the British army. The captain of the *Chesapeake* turned him down. In response, the *Leopard* fired three shots into the sides of the *Chesapeake*. Three men died and eighteen

This engraving depicts the conflict between the *Chesapeake* and the *Leopard*. The captain of the *Leopard* was searching for four deserters in particular. After overwhelming the *Chesapeake*, British naval officers found the deserters on board. They were arrested and taken to Halifax, Canada, to be tried.

were hurt. The American public was outraged. President Jefferson ordered all British warships out of American waters.

# Caught in the Crossfire

Meanwhile, fighting between Great Britain and France was heating up. England and France passed decrees that said that they would seize the goods and/or ships of anyone trading with the other. American merchant ships were caught in the middle. Hundreds of American ships were seized. In response, the United States government passed an embargo. No American-made goods were allowed to leave America. The United States had hoped to hurt England and France economically by not trading with them at all.

# CALHOUN BUILDS A REPUTATION

After the *Chesapeake* affair, cities and towns across the United States held meetings to protest British actions. Calhoun's hometown of Abbeville, South Carolina, held one of these meetings in its courthouse. Calhoun was named to the committee in charge of writing and presenting the protest resolutions for the town. In the resolutions, which he presented on August 3, 1807, Calhoun recommended that the militia be prepared for war. He also sided with Virginians who had rioted to protest the attack. The people of Abbeville were very impressed with his speech. His new law practice and his political career in the years to come would benefit greatly from the reputation he gained from this experience.

The embargo backfired. The American economy suffered as a result. John Randolph, who was against the embargo, said it was like trying "to cure corns by cutting off the toes," as quoted in *The War of 1812: A Forgotten Conflict,* by Donald R. Hickey. Though America suffered greatly, England and France did not. The embargo lasted one year and three months.

In March 1809, the government ended the embargo and started the Nonintercourse Act. Under this act, American merchants could not trade with England or France. The next year, Congress passed another bill, which said that America would end trade with either France or England if the other lifted its restrictions on American merchants. France responded by promising to lift restrictions on the United States

James Madison was not enthusiastic about going to war. However, he felt he could not ignore the will of Congress, many of the members of which were elected because they wanted to declare war on England. Madison was the fourth president of the United States. He served between 1809 and 1817.

if it stopped trading with England. England would not lift its restrictions until France lifted its for all countries, not just the United States.

James Madison, who was then president, convinced Congress to pass a Nonimportation Act against England in February 1811. Under the act, British goods could not be imported to the United States. Relations between America and England continued to worsen. The U.S. government had hoped that the Nonimportation Act would hurt England's economy enough that its government would be willing to end its trade restrictions. However, England would not lift its restrictions until France ended its decrees. Neither side was willing to compromise.

The Nonimportation Act was not the only source of trouble. An American ship, *President*, fought with a smaller British ship, HMS *Little Belt*, off the coast of the United States. Nine crew members of the *Little Belt* were killed and twenty-three were injured. Many Americans were pleased by this event. They saw it as revenge for the

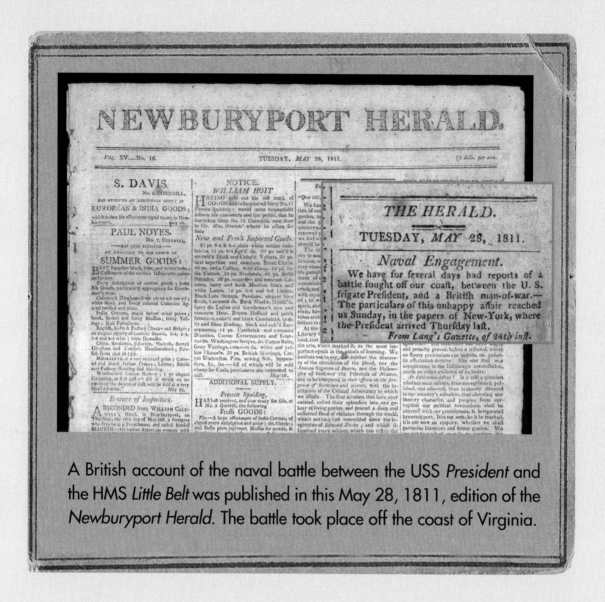

A British account of the naval battle between the USS *President* and the HMS *Little Belt* was published in this May 28, 1811, edition of the *Newburyport Herald*. The battle took place off the coast of Virginia.

*Chesapeake* affair. British citizens saw the fight as an unprovoked attack by Americans. Many British people called for revenge.

Conflicts between settlers and Native Americans in the West also created problems. As American settlers tried to push farther west, fighting between them and the Native Americans increased. Many of these Native Americans were supported by the British. This turned more Americans against England and in favor of war. Republicans also hoped to stop the British from supporting the Native Americans in any way, helping to end the fighting and allowing the United States to claim more land in the West.

# A Call to War

All of these events led directly to President Madison asking Congress to meet early. On November 4, 1811, the twelfth Congress met in Washington, D.C. Seated in that Congress were John Calhoun and John Randolph.

The twelfth Congress was Calhoun's first congressional session. Henry Clay was the Speaker of the House. Clay, Calhoun, and several other younger men from the South were known as the war hawks because of their eagerness to go to war with England. With an eye toward war, Clay selected Calhoun, among other war hawks, to be a member of the House Committee on Foreign Relations. Though Calhoun had just entered Congress, he was placed in the number two spot on the committee.

The day after the session started, Congress received a letter from President Madison. In the letter, Madison wrote that England had made "war on our lawful commerce." He suggested that the nation start making preparations for war. The letter was given to the Foreign Relations Committee. Calhoun worked closely with the committee's chairman, Peter Porter, to address President Madison's letter. In fact, Calhoun wrote most of the report. On November 29, 1811, the committee gave its report to Congress. In it, the committee chastised England for continuing to seize American sailors, ships, and goods. The committee asked that Congress start preparing the nation for war. The report proposed the following resolutions:

1. Resolved, That the military establishment, as authorized by existing laws, ought to be immediately completed, by filling up the ranks and prolonging the enlistments of the troops: and that, to encourage enlistments, a bounty in lands be given, in addition to the pay and bounty now allowed by law.

2. That an additional force of ten thousand regular troops ought to be immediately raised, to serve for three years; and that a bounty in lands ought to be given to encourage enlistments.

3. That it is expedient to authorize the President, under proper regulations, to accept the service of any number of volunteers, not exceeding fifty thousand, to be organized, trained, and held in readiness to act on such service as the exigences of the Government may require.

4. That the President be authorized to order out, from time to time, such detachments of the militia as, in his opinion, the public service may require.

5. That all the vessels not now in service, belonging to the navy, and worthy of repair be immediately filled up and put in commission.

6. That it is expedient to permit our merchant vessels, owned exclusively by resident citizens, and commanded and navigated solely by citizens, to arm, under proper regulations to be prescribed by law, in self-defence, against the unlawful proceedings against them on the high seas.

## CHAPTER 3

# RANDOLPH OPPOSES THE PUSH FOR WAR

Not everyone was in support of going to war with England. The Republican Party was split. Many who decided to vote for the Foreign Relations Committee resolutions hoped that war preparations would help avoid war. Many Republicans did not believe that the country could win another war against England. Others thought the war was simply unnecessary.

The man leading this opposition was John Randolph. From the start, Randolph was against taking any action over commerce. He viewed problems with trade as an issue with which the government should not be involved. Randolph had bitterly opposed the embargo of 1807. He thought that it was unconstitutional, and he was outraged by the damage it had done to the Virginia economy. He felt that merchants should be armed and able to defend themselves against attackers. This was the only element of the Foreign Relations Committee report with which he agreed. On December 10, 1811, Randolph took the floor of the House of Representatives to deliver his speech against the report and war with England.

Randolph was known for his sharp tongue and biting comments, especially when he was opposed to something. He often spoke with the self-assurance of someone who knew he was right, and because of this, he was usually unyielding. On this occasion, Randolph lived up to his reputation.

# Arguments Against Going to War

Wasting little time on the formalities with which congressmen of the era typically began their speeches, Randolph quickly called into question the authority and motives of his colleagues on the Foreign Relations Committee: "On what ground . . . they felt themselves authorized . . . to recommend the raising of standing armies, with a view (as had been declared) of immediate war—a war not of defense, but of conquest, of aggrandizement, of ambition; a war foreign to the interest of this country, to the interest of humankind."

This was a loaded charge. Not only did Randolph dismiss the war hawks' assertion that the options facing the country were between war and peace, but he also addressed rumors that the war resolutions were the result of political calculations and a thirst for more land.

It was widely suspected that political ambition was a leading force behind the Republicans' push for war. They hoped to unite the party against a common enemy and silence their critics, namely the Federalists, who the Republicans thought would become unpopular for opposing the war. Further, many Republicans thought that war would make it easy to force the British into compromise. Elections would be held in 1812, and Republicans hoped to have the public on their side if all went according to plan.

Randolph was not so sure that the Republicans' war plans would be as popular as they hoped. He warned his fellow Republicans that the

Federalists had built a standing army—something he was adamantly against—in their years as a majority in Congress and they had also fallen out of favor with the American public.

Randolph scorned his colleagues' talk of invading British-ruled Canada—which, though not included in the report, was gleefully talked about by the war hawks—as a greedy drive for land. He referred to the idea as "a dangerous experiment" that couldn't be pulled off with the ease that the war hawks had convinced themselves was possible. He remarked sarcastically that "it seems this is to be a holiday campaign—there is to be

These are pages from the congressional record from John Randolph's December 10, 1811, speech in which he opposed the war resolutions. Randolph complained of being exhausted before he began his address and even tried to coax some of his colleagues to speak before him to give him some time to gather his thoughts.

no expense of blood, or treasure, on our part—Canada is to conquer herself." He warned that an assault on Canada would leave the Chesapeake Bay and other ports and harbors undefended.

Further, Randolph warned that Americans would not be in full support of a war over trade since only merchants and contractors would benefit from the war. "Our people will not submit to be taxed for this war of conquest," he said. It is "the people," Randolph cried, "their blood, their taxes, that must . . . support it."

Randolph also had a hatred for Napoléon Bonaparte and his attempts to take over other countries. He worried that war with England would put the United States "in common cause with France." Moreover, Randolph warned that going to war with England while it was also fighting France endangered America further. If England were to lose the war with France, France would be "in possession of the British naval power." He cautioned that by waging war with England, the United States was in danger of becoming "a party to [Bonaparte's] views, a partner in his wars."

Randolph pleaded with the war hawks to reconsider their position. He reminded them of the promises they made when they came to power to lower taxes, pay off the national debt, and limit the size of the military. Those promises would be broken should they vote for war. Randolph's speech was a passionate appeal for the war hawks to think about the possible costs of the war, not just the possible gains.

Randolph ended his speech by apologizing for it, claiming that it often strayed from the subject. The sickness he had contracted as a young man had never left him and got worse from time to time. He blamed the "wild manner" of his speech on this sickness. However, he said that he hoped that Congress might find "some method . . . in his madness."

## CHAPTER 4

# CALHOUN DEFENDS THE WAR RESOLUTIONS

On December 12, 1811, John Calhoun gave his own speech to the House of Representatives. It was the first major speech of his congressional career. In it, he directly addressed the speech that Randolph had made two days earlier. Though Calhoun may have been nervous about being such a young man addressing older, more respected congressmen, he did not show it. He coolly laid out his position and what he believed were the pressing needs to prepare for war.

## Arguments for War

First, Calhoun addressed Randolph's criticism that there was no just cause for war. He listed the seizing of sailors, ships, and goods and the restriction of trade as acts of aggression. Calhoun said that America's attempts to negotiate a peaceful end to these problems had become "hopeless." "The evil still grows . . . which shall we do," he asked, "abandon or defend our own commercial and maritime rights, and the personal liberties of our citizens?" Calhoun accused Randolph of wanting America to submit to England. He argued that America had to fight or be ruled by England once again.

# The Calhoun-Randolph Debate on the Eve of the War of 1812

Many opponents of the war feared that the country was unprepared for another conflict with England. Calhoun suggested that that should be changed as soon as possible, as the Foreign Relations Committee had asked in its report. He also accused those who had been in Congress longer, including Randolph, of failing to see that the country was properly defended. He said:

> If our country is unprepared, let us remedy the evil as soon as possible. Let the gentleman submit his plan; and, if a reasonable one, I doubt not it will be supported by the House. But, sir, let us admit

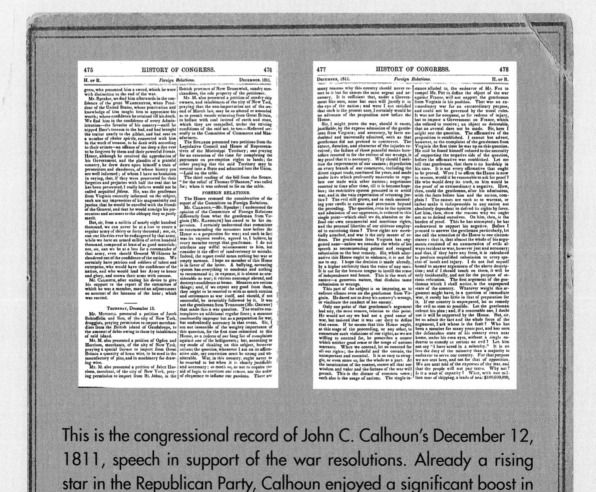

This is the congressional record of John C. Calhoun's December 12, 1811, speech in support of the war resolutions. Already a rising star in the Republican Party, Calhoun enjoyed a significant boost in popularity after delivering this successful address.

the fact and the whole force of the argument, I ask whose is the fault? Who has been a member for many years past, and has seen the defenceless state of his country even near home, under his own eyes, without a single endeavor to remedy so serious an evil? Let him not say "I have acted in a minority." It is no less the duty of the minority than a majority to endeavor to serve our country. For that purpose we are sent here, and not for that of opposition.

Calhoun next addressed Randolph's claim that Americans would not support the war and would resent having to pay taxes to finance it. "Why not?" he asked. "If taxes become necessary, I do not hesitate to say the people will pay cheerfully. It is for their Government and their cause, and it would be their interest and duty to pay it." Calhoun went on to say that he did not feel that the people would feel that the rights of merchants were not worth defending or that "the defence would cost more than the gain." Calhoun suggested that waging war on England for its actions on merchants would make the nation safer, stronger, and wealthier. According to Calhoun, this war was for national independence, not economic gain.

Calhoun dismissed Randolph's argument against having a standing army. He did not think that raising the number of troops to oppose a specific threat was a standing army. He said, "I think a regular force, raised for a period of actual hostilities, cannot be called a standing army. There is a just distinction between such a force, and one raised as a peace establishment." He also felt that the payment offered to soldiers would persuade young men to join the army and fight for their country.

Calhoun rejected Randolph's claim that invading and perhaps taking over Canada was based on greed and not defense. Instead, Calhoun saw Canada as a legitimate target since it was ruled by England, which had attacked the United States. He showed Randolph's argument to be ridiculous by saying: "By his system, if you receive a blow on the breast, you dare not return it on the head; you are obliged to measure and return it on the precise point on which it was received. If you do not do so with mathematical accuracy, it ceases to be self-defence; it becomes an unprovoked attack."

Calhoun also disagreed with Randolph's argument that the United States would be allying itself with France by waging war with England. He questioned whether America should ignore its own interests in order to protect another country's interests. Further, Calhoun suggested that if England stopped attacking American interests, then war would not be waged. He said:

> The balance of power has also been introduced as an argument for submission. England is said to be a barrier against the military despotism of France . . . this argument of the balance of power is well calculated for the British Parliament, but not at all fitted to the American Congress. Tell them that they have to contend with this mighty power, and that if they persist in insult and injury to the American people, they will compel them to throw the whole weight of their force into the scale of the enemy.

Point by point, Calhoun had torn down Randolph's arguments. Calhoun's Republican supporters cheered his sharp and spirited response to Randolph, who may have been unaccustomed to being so soundly rebuked, especially by a newcomer. Calhoun's performance raised his already high profile in Congress, especially among war hawk Republicans.

+≡= **CHAPTER 5** =≡+

# THE WAR YEARS

F ollowing the House debates, the Foreign Relations Committee's resolutions were passed, and preparations for war advanced. For the war hawks, the question was not war or peace, but war or submission. As Calhoun had outlined, many feared that if the British were allowed to continue trampling on Americans' rights without any fearful response, then nothing would stop them from trying to take over the United States. For many, the upcoming war was fast becoming a second war of independence. This war would allow America to rid itself once and for all of the threat of a British takeover.

## War Preparations

The debate between Calhoun and Randolph continued as the nation prepared for war. When Congress voted to pass a ninety-day embargo, the men were once again on opposite sides. The embargo passed in an effort to keep American merchants safe in port if war was declared. However, news of the embargo leaked out before it was officially announced— some think by Randolph—and merchants fled American ports to try to make extra money. Many merchants were not worried about a declaration of war. They didn't think it would happen. Embargos and other acts had been passed for years in the hopes of making England change its ways, and no war had ever been declared. Rumors circled that told of further attempts to make treaties with Great Britain. Though Congress had voted to make the army larger, a lack of funds kept it from achieving its goal of 10,000 men. Moreover, congressmen were still voting for the embargo and for further preparations, thinking that war would be avoided. Few truly expected the nation to go to war.

Calhoun and Randolph sparred throughout the congressional session, right up to the final vote for war. Randolph tried to get Congress to agree to delay the vote until October 1812. He hoped that if the country had to go to war it would be more prepared by then, and he felt that the weather in late fall would make sailing more difficult for England. As the months wore on, his arguments became increasingly desperate. He even argued that a passing comet and an eclipse were signs that going to war would be wrong. Calhoun grimly dismissed his claim. On May 29, Randolph was ruled out of order while he was making another of his long speeches to stop the march to war. It was the first time in twelve years in Congress that one of Randolph's speeches had been cut short. An angry Randolph replied with a letter to the people of Virginia, whom he represented. The letter detailed much of the text of his speech. It was his last major effort to stop the war.

On June 1, 1812, President Madison sent a letter recommending war with Great Britain to Congress. Calhoun was essential to writing the war bill, which he presented to the House of Representatives on June 3, 1812. In it, he again expressed the war hawks' feeling that England left the United States with no choice but to fight or surrender its rights.

## A MATTER OF TIMING

If Congress had waited until October, as Randolph recommended, war might have been avoided. In early 1812, the British had started paying more respect to American ships and sailors. Many British ships were ordered to take special care not to fight with American ships or take American citizens from their ships. British ships were also staying clear of American waters to avoid any conflict. The British announced that they would end their trade restrictions on America on June 16, 1812. The news did not reach America for two weeks. By then, war had already been declared. If communications during 1811 had been faster, the War of 1812 might have never happened.

# War Is Declared

The bill passed in the House of Representatives in two days, and in the Senate, after much wrangling, in two weeks. It was the closest vote on a war bill in United States history. Almost 40 percent of congressmen who voted cast their vote against the war. On June 18, 1812, a day after the bill cleared the Senate, President Madison declared war on England.

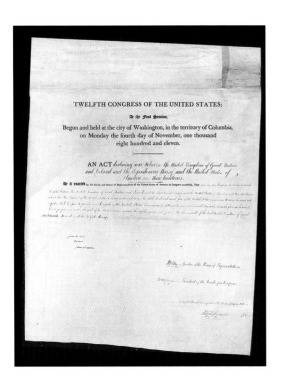

This is the congressional act declaring war against Great Britain in 1812. The U.S. Constitution gives Congress the power to declare war and assigns the president to command the troops once they are committed to battle. Nevertheless, many presidents commit troops to action without asking Congress to formally declare war.

After war was declared on England, the members of the United States Congress worked to pass bills that they thought would help during wartime. These included a bill banning the trade of war-related goods with Canada and another placing a heavy tax on imported goods. The tax bill passed despite much protest from Federalists, who felt that the taxes would more strongly affect those in the Northeast—where Federalism and antiwar sentiment were strongest—since they had more ports.

# Public Reaction to the War

Most people in the United States were surprised to hear that war had finally been declared against England. Federalists around the country reacted to the news of the war with sadness and fear. Many in New England closed their shops and flew their flags at half-mast. Federalists in the government vowed to do everything within their power to act against the war. Many Republicans saw this opposition as a threat to the United States. They thought that those who had been

Andrew Jackson was a general of the United States Army during the War of 1812. Under his leadership, the United States defeated the British in the Battle of New Orleans on January 8, 1815. This portrait shows him in uniform and on horseback on a battlefield in Alabama.

opposed to war before should support their country now that war had been declared. Many Republicans voiced their feelings that those who were against the war were also against the United States. Tempers flared between antiwar Federalists and pro-war Republicans. In Baltimore, rioting broke out. Hundreds of people stormed a Federalist newspaper building. Many people were hurt and killed. Though the violence had erupted out of a hope to stop the Federalists from speaking out against the war, it had the opposite effect. People around the country sympathized with the Federalists, and antiwar feelings grew.

# An Unprepared Army

As Randolph and others against the war had feared, the U.S. Army was not as prepared for war at the start of the hostilities as many had hoped it to be. Many in the army were inexperienced and not well trained. Soldiers started deserting at a high rate. In response, Congress increased the amount of money and land that those who joined the army would receive. Before the end of the war, soldiers in the U.S. Army were promised 320 acres (129 hectares) of land and $124 just for joining—that was more than most people made in two years at that

BATTLE OF PLATTSBURG.

This hand-colored engraving depicts the Battle of Plattsburgh, which took place in September 1814. British troops invaded the United States from Canada on September 1, and advanced to Plattsburgh, New York. American forces under the command of Lieutenant Thomas Macdonough defeated them on September 11.

time. Despite Congress's efforts to make the army better, funding was still very poor. Troops in battle often had to wait months for shoes, clothing, blankets, and other necessary supplies. Much of the food they received was bad. Soldiers often did not get paid for months at a time. Some soldiers refused to fight until they got their money.

The first battles on land did not go as well as Calhoun and the war hawks had thought they would. Attempts to invade Canada failed. American troops surrendered several major forts and hundreds of men to the British and Native Americans. This was due in part to the fact that the army had poor leadership and also because many members of state militias would not cross the border into Canada.

By contrast, the sea battles went better than expected. England had had the best navy in the world for the past 100 years. It had 1,000 ships in its navy. The United States had only 17 ships and was having trouble recruiting sailors to run them. Luckily, England was more focused on its war with France than with the United States and at first did not send many ships to fight the United States. American captains and sailors also proved themselves to be able opponents against the British. The United States won many key naval battles in the first year of the War of 1812.

# England Steps Up Its Campaign

Many things changed in 1813. Faced with several defeats at sea, England sent more ships to fight America. As a result, the United States had many more losses at sea. However, the young soldiers who were untrained in 1812 were now becoming more skilled, and the United States started winning more land battles.

Changes were happening in Congress as well. An election was held in which many Republicans lost their seats in Congress. Randolph lost his seat in the House of Representatives in 1813. The Federalists continued to try to limit the war. Calhoun, who was reelected, was again drawn into many debates to defend the war.

At top, a British cartoon portraying President James Madison and his secretary of war fleeing Washington as the buildings behind them burn. At bottom, a drawing showing the ruins of the U.S. Capitol after it was burned by British troops. American troops had earlier burned public buildings in Canada.

On April 11, 1814, Napoléon Bonaparte was exiled from France, and there was peace in Europe. This peace allowed England to concentrate its efforts on the United States. It started shipping more troops to the United States. British soldiers occupied Maine and invaded the Chesapeake Bay. On August 24, 1814, British troops took over Washington, D.C. President Madison was forced to flee the White House. British troops ate his dinner, which had been left on the table, before they burned the White House. Though they left the following day, they had done a lot of damage to the city.

The United States was in a crisis. Congressmen returned to Washington to meet in September. Men were still deserting the army in high numbers, and there were not enough soldiers to protect the nation's borders. The economy was in a terrible state largely because of trade restrictions. Many Republicans had lost confidence in President Madison. Congress worked to solve the nation's crisis. It passed several bills to increase the number of troops and shore up the economy.

# Peace Treaty

Meanwhile, peace talks were taking place between England and the United States in Ghent, Belgium. On December 24, 1814, a treaty was signed. England and the United States agreed to restore the land that each country had held before the war, leave each other's territory, release prisoners of war, and stop taking goods from enemy ships. The United States also promised to restore the rights and possessions to the Native Americans that they had before the war and to make efforts to end the slave trade.

The Treaty of Ghent did not address any of the issues for which the United States had declared war, however. No mention was made of England's practice of taking American sailors or restricting trade. The concessions that Calhoun and the war hawks thought England would give to the United States so easily were not even mentioned in the final

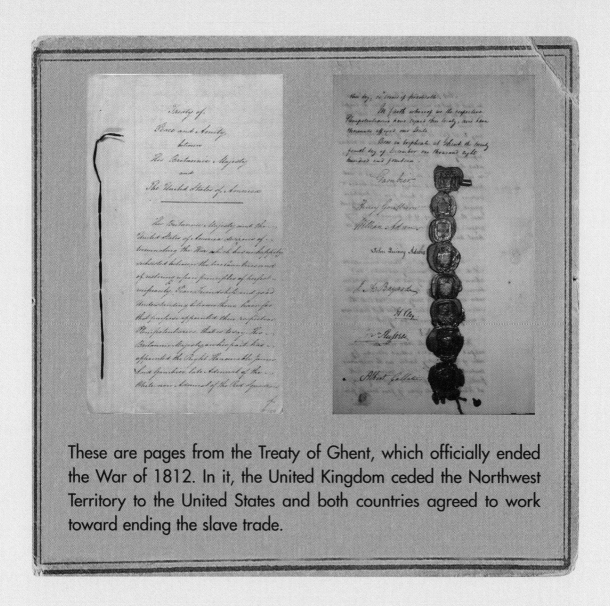

These are pages from the Treaty of Ghent, which officially ended the War of 1812. In it, the United Kingdom ceded the Northwest Territory to the United States and both countries agreed to work toward ending the slave trade.

document. The treaty was taken from Ghent to Washington, D.C. It arrived there on February 11, 1815. It was passed in Congress on February 15, 1815. The war officially ended on February 17, 1815, when the United States and England exchanged the ratified treaty.

During the time that the Treaty of Ghent was being negotiated, battles raged in New Orleans. The final battle took place on January 8, 1815, two weeks after the Treaty of Ghent had been signed. The British lost two generals and about 2,000 men on that day. The Americans lost only about seventy men. Many Americans saw this major loss for the British as an overall victory in the war.

## CHAPTER 6

# AFTER THE WAR

At the end of the war, it became apparent that both Calhoun's and Randolph's arguments in the debate had merit. Although the United States' original war goals were not met in the peace treaty, many Americans claimed victory. England never again took soldiers from American ships, and it stopped restricting American trade once the war had ended. The United States had won a level of respect with England and throughout Europe as a result of the War of 1812.

Congress voted to increase the army to 10,000 men and build new ships for the navy during the peace following the War of 1812. Republicans began to adopt the long-held Federalist policy of avoiding war by preparing for it. The standing army that Randolph was against now became an ideal.

The perceived success of the war also helped to unite the Republican Party. Although it did not meet its war goals, the public was satisfied that the United States did not have to surrender. The Republican Party was stronger than ever. The Federalist Party was disbanded several years later.

Although many Americans saw the War of 1812 as a success, many of John Randolph's debate points were proved true. The war hawks had gone into war before the army was prepared for battle. The cost of war was much higher than anyone had expected. The national debt almost tripled. If the war had continued much longer than it did, the United States could have possibly gone bankrupt. Randolph's warnings that Canada would not fall easily were also correct. The War of 1812 actually became an important uniting force for Canadians. Before the war, Canada was made up of several separate groups of people. After the war, Canada was a united country, determined to remain so.

The debate over the War of 1812 was the first of several debates between John C. Calhoun and John Randolph. Randolph was reelected to the House of Representatives in 1815. After the War of 1812, the country was in a difficult financial situation.

When the embargoes and restrictions on trade were lifted, England once again traded with America. Its products were cheaper and of a higher quality than similar American products. American businesses could not compete. In 1816, Congress tried to pass a tariff bill to tax goods coming into America that its businesses could produce. Calhoun was in favor of the tariff. He thought the money raised by the tariffs should be used to build roads and canals. He claimed that these improvements would make the nation stronger. He also supported a strong federal government. Randolph argued against the tariff bill, saying that it put "an immense tax on one portion of the community to put money into the pockets of another." He was afraid that most improvements from the money from the tariffs would be made in the North, where most manufacturers were. He also worried that the South would be unable to export its cotton if the tariffs hurt relations between the United States and other countries. Further, he saw this tariff and other laws as the federal government trampling on states'

This print shows John Calhoun *(left)* at a ball celebrating the ninth anniversary of the Battle of New Orleans. At right is President John Quincy Adams, whose wife Louisa hosted the ball. Also depicted are Daniel Webster *(second from left)*, Andrew Jackson *(center)*, and Henry Clay *(second from right)*.

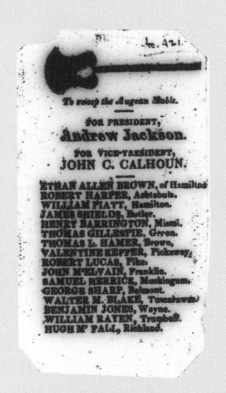

This 1828 election ticket shows John Calhoun as the vice presidential candidate in Andrew Jackson's successful bid for the presidency. It also lists a number of Ohio delegates for Jackson.

rights. He was opposed to a federal government with more power than the states, saying, "I am not for a policy which must end in the destruction, and speedy destruction, too, of the whole of the state governments." The tariff passed, but the debate did not end.

Calhoun became vice president of the United States in 1825. As vice president, he presided over the Senate. Randolph was elected to the Senate in 1825. Randolph maintained his position against tariffs and in favor of states' rights. Calhoun, who had seen the economy suffer in his home state of South Carolina, reconsidered his position on tariffs. Calhoun also began to side with Randolph on states' rights issues. The two men who had once argued with each other so hotly were now on the same side of a debate. When a higher tariff was passed in 1832, Calhoun argued that the Constitution gave the states the right to nullify, or reject, federal laws that they think are unconstitutional. South Carolina passed an ordinance of nullification, which said that the tariff laws were unconstitutional. This was the beginning of the difficulties between the Northern and Southern states that would ultimately lead to the Civil War.

Randolph's congressional career had ended in 1829, but he continued to serve as a voice for states' rights until he died on May 24, 1833. Calhoun was to follow in Randolph's footsteps as the leading force in America for states' rights and a limited federal government.

# CALHOUN MAKES HIS BREAK

During Calhoun's time as vice president, he came under criticism for not ending some of Randolph's lengthy speeches against actions taken by Henry Clay and President John Quincy Adams. Randolph's speeches would last up to six hours. Through all of Randolph's ranting, Calhoun never interrupted. Many senators accused Calhoun of trying to hurt the administration by allowing Randolph to keep making his speeches. This led to a public debate in the newspaper, which took place between Calhoun and an anonymous writer, whom many thought might have been President Adams. It was during this time that Calhoun made his first breaks from the Republican administration and became more aligned with his former opponent.

In the later years of his career, Calhoun's major battle for states' rights was in defense of slavery. He, like Randolph before him, did not believe that the federal government should be able to pass laws against slavery. He felt that it would hurt the Southern states to outlaw slavery and that it was a state's right to allow slavery or not. Until his death, Calhoun would not compromise on the issue of states' rights. Though his views became increasingly unpopular, he was well known and respected for his strong will and determination. The man who had led the country to change and the War of 1812 now clung to many of the ideals and values that Randolph had once defended so passionately. Calhoun worked in the government until his death on March 31, 1850.

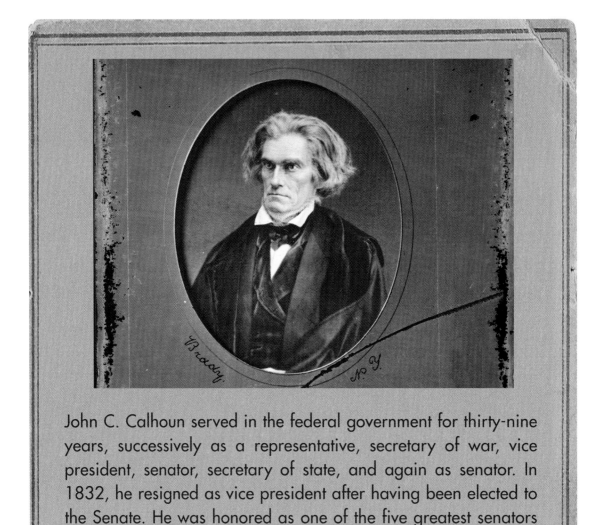

John C. Calhoun served in the federal government for thirty-nine years, successively as a representative, secretary of war, vice president, senator, secretary of state, and again as senator. In 1832, he resigned as vice president after having been elected to the Senate. He was honored as one of the five greatest senators of all time by the members of the Senate in 1957.

Since the time of their great debates, Randolph and Calhoun have become unpopular due to their pro-slavery beliefs. John Randolph has disappeared from most history books, and his fiery speeches and important debates have been forgotten by most Americans. Today, Calhoun is most remembered for his views in favor of states' rights and slavery than for his early career when he sparred with the gentleman from Virginia. The legacy of these two men has not died, though. They fought with all of their might for freedom and for what they believed was the best course for the United States. The debates between John Calhoun and John Randolph helped to define America in war and peace.

## Excerpt of John Randoph's Speech to the House of Representatives on December 10, 1811

It was a question, as it had been presented to the House, of peace or war. In that light it had been argued; in no other light could he consider it, after the declarations made by members of the Committee of Foreign Relations . . . The Committee of Foreign Relations had indeed decided that the subject of arming the militia (which he had pressed upon them an indispensable to the public security) did not come within the scope of their authority. On what ground, he had been and still was unable to see, they had felt themselves authorized (when that subject was before another committee) to recommend the raising of standing armies, with a view (as had been declared) of immediate war—a war not of defence, but of conquest, of aggrandizement, of ambition; a war foreign to the interest of this country, to the interests of humanity itself . . .

He knew not how gentlemen, calling themselves, could advocate such a war. What was their doctrine in 1788–9, when the command of the army—that highest of all possible trusts in any Government, be the form what it may—was reposed in the bosom of the Father of his Country, the sanctuary of a nation's love, the only hope that never came in vain! . . .

Those who opposed the army then, were indeed denounced as the partisans of France; as the same men—some of them at least—are now held up as the advocates of England; those firm and undeviating Republicans, who then dared, and now dare, to cling to the ark of the Constitution, to defend it even at the expense of their wild projects of mad ambition! There was a fatality attending plenitude of power. Soon or late, some mania seizes upon its possessors—they fall from the dizzy height through the giddiness of their own heads. Like a vast estate, heaped up by the labor and industry of one man, which seldom survives the third generation—power, gained by patient assiduity, by a faithful and regular discharge of its attendant duties, soon gets above its own origin. Intoxicated with their own greatness the Federal party fell. Will not the same causes produce the same effects now, as then? Sir, you may raise this army, you may build up this vast structure of patronage, this mighty apparatus of favoritism; but—"lay not the flattering unction to your souls"—you will never live to enjoy the succession. You sign your political death warrant . . .

This war of conquest, a war for the acquisition of territory and subjects, is to be a new commentary on the doctrine that Republics are destitute of ambition—that they are addicted to peace, wedded to the happiness and safety of the great body of their people. But it seems this is to be a holiday campaign—there is to be no expense of blood, or treasure, on our part—Canada is to conquer herself—she is to be subdued by the principles of fraternity. The people of that country are first to be seduced from their allegiance, and converted into traitors, as preparatory to the making them good citizens. Although he must acknowledge that some of our flaming patriots were thus manufactured, he did not think the process would hold good with a whole community. It was a dangerous experiment. We were to succeed in the French mode by the system of fraternity—all is French! But how dreadfully it might be retorted on the Southern and Western slaveholding States. He detested this subornation of treason. No—if he must have them, let them fall by the valor of our, by fair, legitimate conquest; not become the victims of treacherous seduction. . .

Our people will not submit to be taxed for this war of conquest and dominion. The Government of the United States was not calculated to wage offensive foreign war—it was instituted for the common defence and general welfare; and whosoever should embark it in a war of offence, would put it to a test which it was by no means calculated to endure. Make it out that Great Britain had instigated the Indians on the late occasion, and he was ready for battle; but not for dominion. He was unwilling, however, under present circumstances, to take Canada, at the risk of the Constitution—to embark in a common cause with France and be dragged at the wheels of a car of some Burr or Bonaparte . . .

And shall Republicans become the instruments of him who has effaced the title of Attila to the "Scourge of God!" Yet even Attila, in the falling fortunes of civilization, had, no doubt, his advocates, his tools, his minions, his parasites in the very countries that he overran—sons of that soil whereon his horse had trod; where grass could never after grow. If perfectly fresh, Mr. Randolph said, (instead of being as he was—his memory clouded, his intellect stupefied, his strength and spirits exhausted) he could not give utterance to that strong detestation which he felt towards (above all other works of the creation) such characters as Zingis, Tamerlane, Kubla-Khan, or Bonaparte. His instincts involuntarily revolted at their bare idea. Malefactors of the human race, who ground down man to a mere machine of their impious and bloody ambition. Yet under all the accumulated wrongs and insults and robberies of the last of these chieftains, are we not in point of fact about to become a party to his views, a party in his wars?

But before this miserable force of ten thousand men was raised to take Canada, he begged them to look at the state of defence at home—to count the cost of the enterprise before it was set on foot, not when it might be too late—when the best blood of the country should be spilt, and nought but empty coffers left to pay the cost? It might lessen his repugnance to that part of the system, to granting these lands, not to those miserable wretches who sell themselves to slavery for a few dollars and a glass of gin, but in fact to the clerks in our offices, some of whom, with an income of fifteen hundred or two thousand dollars, lived at the rate of four or five thousand, and yet grew rich—who perhaps at that moment were making out blank assignments for these land rights.

He would beseech the House, before they ran their heads against this post, Quebec, to count the cost. His word for it, Virginia planters would not be taxed to support such a war—a war which must aggravate their present distresses; in which they had not the remotest interest . . .

He called upon those professing to be Republicans to make good the promises held out by their Republican predecessors when they came into power—promises, which for years afterwards they had honestly, faithfully fulfilled. We had vaunted of paying off the national debt, of retrenching useless establishments; and yet had now become as infatuated with standing armies, loans, taxes, navies, and war, as ever were the Essex Junto. What Republicanism is this?

## Excerpt of John Calhoun's Speech to the House of Representatives on December 12, 1811

Mr. Speaker: I understood the opinion of the Committee of Foreign Relations differently from what the gentleman from Virginia [Mr. Randolph] has stated to be his impression. I certainly understood that committee as recommending the measures now before the House as a preparation for war; and such in fact was its express resolve, agreed to, I believe, by every member except that gentleman. I do not attribute any wilful misstatement to him, but consider it the effect of inadvertency or mistake. Indeed, the report could mean nothing but war or empty menace. I hope no member of this House is in favor of the latter. A bullying, menacing system has everything to condemn and nothing to recommend it; in expense, it is almost as considerable as war; it excites contempt abroad, and destroys confidence at home. Menaces are serious things; and, if we expect any good from them, they ought to be resorted to with as much caution and seriousness as war itself, and should, if not successful, be invariably followed by it . . .

Sir, I might prove the war, should it ensue, justifiable, by the express admission of the gentleman from Virginia; and necessary, by facts undoubted and universally admitted, such as that gentleman did not pretend to controvert. The extent, duration, and character of the injuries received; the failure of those peaceful means heretofore resorted to for the redress of our wrongs, is my proof that it is necessary. Why should I mention the impressment of our seamen; depredation on every branch of our commerce, including the direct export trade, continued for years, and made under laws which professedly undertake to regulate our trade with other nations; negotiation resorted to time after time, till it is become hopeless; the restrictive system persisted in to avoid war, and in the vain expectation of returning justice? The evil still grows, and in each succeeding year swells in extent and pretension beyond the preceding. The question, even in the opinion and admission of our opponents, is reduced to this single point—which shall we do, abandon or defend our commercial and maritime rights and the personal liberties of our citizens employed in exercising them? These rights are essentially attacked, and war is the only means of redress . . .

The first argument of the gentleman which I shall notice, is the unprepared state of the country. Whatever weight this argument might have, in a question of immediate war, it surely has little in that of preparation for it. If our country is unprepared, let us remedy the evil as soon as possible. Let the gentleman submit his plan; and, if a reasonable one, I doubt not it will be supported by the House. But, sir, let us admit the fact and the whole force of the argument, I ask whose is the fault? Who has been a member for many years past, and has seen the defenceless state of his country even near home, under his own eyes, without a single endeavor to remedy so serious an evil? Let him not say "I have acted in a minority." It is no less the duty of the minority than a majority to endeavor to serve our country. For that purpose we are sent here, and not for that of opposition. We are next told of the expenses of the war, and that the people will not pay taxes. Why not? Is it a want of capacity? . . . if taxes become necessary, I do not hesitate to say the people will pay cheerfully. It is for their Government and their cause, and would be their interest and duty to pay it. But it may be, and I believe was said, that the nation will not pay taxes, because the rights violated are not worth defending, or that the defence will cost more than the profit. Sir, I here enter my solemn protest against this low and "calculating avarice" entering this hall of legislation. It is only fit for ships and counting-houses, and ought not to disgrace the seat of sovereignty by its squalid and vile appearance . . .

We are next told of the danger of war! I believe we are all ready to acknowledge its hazards and accidents; but I cannot think we have any extraordinary danger to contend with, at least so much as to warrant an acquiescence in the injuries we have received. On the contrary, I believe no war can be less dangerous to internal peace, or national existence.

Sir, I think a regular force, raised for a period of actual hostilities, cannot be called a standing army. There is a just distinction between such a force, and one raised as a peace establishment. Whatever may be the composition of the latter, I hope the former will consist of some of the best materials of the country. The ardent patriotism of our young men, and the reasonable bounty in land, which is proposed to be given, will impel them to join their country's standard and to fight her battles; they will not forget the citizen in the soldier, and in obeying their officer, learn to condemn their Constitution . . .

I, sir, will now conclude by adverting to an argument of the gentleman from Virginia used in debate on a previous day. He asked why not debate the war immediately. The answer is obvious: because we are not yet prepared. But, says the gentleman, such language as is here held will provoke Great Britain to commence hostilities. I have no such fears. She knows well that such a course would unite all parties here; a thing which above all others she most dreads. Besides, such has been our past conduct, that she will still calculate on our patience and submission until war is actually commenced.

**Editor's Note:** The preceding excerpts are from the official congressional records of John Randoph and John Calhoun's speeches. They contain a combination of direct quotes and more general summaries.

# TIMELINE

**1773** June 2: John Randolph is born.

**1782** March 18: John Calhoun is born.

**1799** March 4: John Randolph begins serving his first term in the United States House of Representatives.

**1811** February: United States passes Nonimportation Act against England.

November 4: Twelfth Congress meets. John Calhoun enters Congress.

November 29: House of Representatives Foreign Relations Committee gives report to Congress recommending that the United States start preparing for war against England.

December 10: Randolph delivers speech against war with England to House of Representatives.

December 12: Calhoun gives speech in defense of war with England.

**1812** June 18: War of 1812 begins.

**1814**    August 24: British troops invade Washington, D.C.

December 24: Treaty of Ghent is signed.

**1815**    February 17: War of 1812 is officially ended.

**1825**    February 9: Calhoun becomes vice president of the United States.

**1833**    May 24: John Randolph dies.

**1850**    March 31: John Calhoun dies.

# GLOSSARY

**desert** To leave the army illegally.

**Federalist Party** An early political party in the United States that was for a strong federal government.

**negotiate** To attempt to arrive at a settlement between two or more parties.

**Nonimportation Act** An act passed by Congress wherein the United States forbid the importation of goods from England.

**Nonintercourse Act** An act passed by Congress wherein no trade was allowed between the United States and England or France.

**nullification** The action of a state to try to stop the operation or enforcement of U.S. federal law.

**ordinance** An order or decree.

**privateer** An armed private ship that is commissioned to cruise against the warships of an enemy.

**Quasi-War** Fighting between France and the United States that took place in the Caribbean between 1798 and 1800.

**ratify** To formally approve.

**Republican Party** A political party in favor of the people having the most power and a restricted federal government.

**unconstitutional** Against the rights laid out in the Constitution of the United States.

# FOR MORE INFORMATION

**Fort McHenry National Monument and Historic Shrine**
2400 East Fort Avenue
Baltimore, MD 21230
(410) 962-4290, ext. 236

**General Society of the War of 1812**
1219 Charmuth Road
Lutherville, MD 21093-6404
http://www.societyofthewarof1812.org

**National Society of the U.S. Daughters of 1812**
1461 Rhode Island Avenue NW
Washington, DC 20005
(202) 745-1812
http://www.usdaughters1812.org

**U.S. National Archives and Records**
700 Pennsylvania Avenue NW
Washington, DC 20408
(866) 272-6272
http://www.archives.gov

# Web Sites

Due to the changing nature of Internet links, the Rosen Publishing Group, Inc., has developed an online list of Web sites related to the subject of this book. This site is updated regularly. Please use this link to access the list:

http://www.rosenlinks.com/ghds/crde

# FOR FURTHER READING

Beyer, Mark. *The War of 1812: The New American Nation Goes to War with England*. New York: Rosen Publishing Group, 2003.

Collier, Christopher, and James Lincoln Collier. *The Jeffersonian Republicans: The Louisiana Purchase and the War of 1812: 1800–1823*. Salt Lake City: Benchmark Books, 1998.

Gillem-Robinet, Harriette. *Washington City Is Burning*. New York: Atheneum, 1996.

King, David C. *New Orleans*. New York: Twenty-First Century Books, 1998.

Livesey, Robert. *The Defenders*. Markham, Ontario, Canada: Stoddart Kids, 1999.

Marrin, Albert. *1812: The War Nobody Won*. New York: Atheneum, 1985.

Smolinski, Diane, and Henry Smolinski. *Battles of the War of 1812* (Americans at War). Chicago: Heinemann Library, 2002.

# BIBLIOGRAPHY

Cheek, H. Lee, ed. *John C. Calhoun: Selected Writings and Speeches.* Washington, DC: Regnery Publishing, 2003.

Durwood, Thomas A., and Teresa Celsi. *John C. Calhoun and the Roots of War.* Englewood Cliffs, NJ: Silver Burdett Press, 1991.

Marquette, Scott. *War of 1812.* Vero Beach, FL: Rourke Publishing, 2002.

Shorey, Kenneth, ed. *Collected Letters of John Randolph of Roanoke to Dr. John Brockenbrough, 1812–1833.* Somerset, NJ: Transaction Publishers, 1988.

# PRIMARY SOURCE IMAGE LIST

**Page 4 (left):** Portrait of John C. Calhoun, circa 1822, created by Charles Bird King. Housed at the Corcoran Gallery of Art in Washington, D.C.

**Page 4 (right):** Portrait of John Randolph, oil painting, 1811. Created by John Wesley Jarvis. Housed at the National Portrait Gallery of the Smithsonian Institution in Washington, D.C.

**Page 7:** Portrait of Thomas Jefferson, lithograph by Henry R. Robinson. Created between 1840 and 1851. Housed at the Library of Congress Prints and Photographs Division in Washington, D.C.

**Page 19:** Portrait of James Madison, engraving by David Edwin. Created between 1809 and 1817. Housed at the Library of Congress Prints and Photographs Division in Washington, D.C.

**Page 20:** "British Account of the Affair between the President, and Little Belt," newspaper article, published in the *Newburyport Herald* in Philadelphia on May 28, 1811.

**Page 25:** Paraphrased transcript of John Randolph's speech to the House of Representatives on December 10, 1811. Housed at the Library of Congress in Washington, D.C.

**Page 28:** Paraphrased transcript of John Calhoun's speech to the House of Representatives on December 12, 1811. Housed at the Library of Congress in Washington, D.C.

**Page 34:** Act of June 18, 1812, 2 STAT 755, Declaration of War with Great Britain, War of 1812. Housed at the U.S. National Archives & Records Administration in Washington, D.C.

**Page 35:** *Andrew Jackson with the Tennessee Forces on the Hickory Grounds (Ala) A.D. 1814*, lithograph, published by William Smith between 1834 and 1835. Housed at the Library of Congress Prints and Photographs Division in Washington, D.C.

**Page 36:** *Battle of Plattsburg*, hand-colored engraving, circa 1814. Housed at the Library of Congress Prints and Photographs Division in Washington, D.C.

**Page 38 (top):** *The Fall of Washington—or Maddy in Full Flight*, cartoon, published in London by S. W. Fores in 1814. Housed at the Library of Congress Prints and Photographs Division in Washington, D.C.

**Page 38 (bottom):** Drawing of the ruins of the U.S. Capitol after British forces burned it. Created by George Munger around 1814. Housed at the Library of Congress Prints and Photographs Division in Washington, D.C.

**Page 40:** The Treaty of Ghent, 1814. Housed at the U.S. National Archives & Records Administration in Washington, D.C.

**Page 44:** "To Sweep the Augean Stable," presidential election ticket for Andrew Jackson and John Calhoun, woodcut with letterpress on woven paper, 1828. Housed at the Library of Congress Rare Book and Special Collections Division in Washington, D.C.

**Page 46:** Portrait of John Calhoun, created between 1855 and 1865. Housed at the Library of Congress Prints and Photographs Division in Washington, D.C.

# INDEX

# About the Author

Jennifer Silate has written more than 100 books for children. She currently lives in Maryland.

# Photo Credits

Cover (left), p. 4 (left) © The Corcoran Gallery of Art/Corbis; cover (right), p. 4 (right) © National Portrait Gallery, Smithsonian Institution; pp. 7, 19, 35, 36, 38, 44, 46 Library of Congress Prints and Photographs Division; p. 10 Picture of Yale University's buildings and grounds, 1716-1980 (RU 703). Manuscripts & Archives, Yale University Library; p. 12 © Getty Images; p. 20 Rosen Publishing Group; p. 17 © The Mariner's Museum, Newport News, VA; pp. 25, 28 Library of Congress, U.S. Congressional Documents and Debates 1774–1875; pp. 34, 40 (left) National Archives and Records Administration; p. 40 (right) Clements Library, University of Michigan; p. 43 © Bettmann/Corbis.

**Designer:** Les Kanturek; **Editor:** Wayne Anderson